MONSTERS

PEGASUS

BY Q.L. PEARCE

KIDHAVEN PRESS
A part of Gale, Cengage Learning

GALE
CENGAGE Learning™

Detroit • New York • San Francisco • New Haven, Conn • Waterville, Maine • London

© 2009 Gale, Cengage Learning

Every effort has been made to trace the owners of copyrighted material.

LIBRARY OF CONGRESS CATALOGING-IN-PUBLICATION DATA

Pearce, Q.L. (Querida Lee)
  Pegasus / by Q.L. Pearce.
    p. cm. — (Monsters)
  Includes bibliographical references and index.
  ISBN 978-0-7377-4082-0 (hardcover)
  1. Pegasus (Greek mythology)—Juvenile literature. I. Title.
  BL820.P4P43 2009
  398'.469—dc22

                            2008033729

KidHaven Press
27500 Drake Rd.
Farmington Hills, MI 48331

ISBN-13: 978-0-7377-4082-0
ISBN-10: 0-7377-4082-5

Printed in the United States of America
1 2 3 4 5 6 7 12 11 10 09 08

CONTENTS

CHAPTER 1

THE BIRTH OF PEGASUS

Horses can run as fast as 40 miles per hour (64kph), but can they fly? At one time, people believed they could. In A.D. 77 a famous Roman historian and **naturalist**, Pliny the Elder, wrote a collection of books about science and nature. In this collection Pliny described flying horses. He claimed that the land south of Egypt along the Red Sea was home to the Pegasi, wild horses that had wings and horns. Many of the animals in Pliny's books were real, but some, like the Pegasi, were myths. A myth is a **traditional** tale that people once believed was true. A myth may include some real places or people, but most of the story is made up.

Greek **mythology** is filled with tales of flying horses. In these myths Zeus was the ruler of the Greek gods. He sometimes traveled in a chariot pulled by the four winds in the form of winged horses. The god of the Sun, Helios, had a stable of ten flying horses. Each day four (sometimes nine) fiery steeds drew him across the sky from east to west. At night Helios and his team returned to his eastern palace in a golden ferryboat.

Ares, the war god, commanded four fire-breathing horses. They could appear wherever there was a battle. Demeter was the goddess of farming and grain. She sometimes took the form of a horse. Demeter was the mother of Arion, a beautiful, winged black stallion. The Greek hero Heracles was the first to ride that **immortal** horse.

In Norse mythology, flying horses pulled the chariot of the Sun. The Sun was the source of heat, but daylight came from the horses' golden manes. Surya, the ancient Hindu Sun god of India, was said to circle the Earth in a chariot of light. Seven flying horses (or one horse with seven heads) drew the vehicle across the sky. Sometimes Surya appeared as a winged horse named Tarkshya.

The most famous flying horse of all is Pegasus. His story is part of Greek mythology. Pegasus was said to be one of the most beautiful creatures in the world. He was often pictured as a snow-white steed with pure white or golden wings. Pegasus was gentle and intelligent. He could inspire people to greatness

In Greek mythology, Pegasus is a snow-white horse with wings.

and was said to have the power to change evil into good. The magical feathers from his wings could give a person wisdom and insight. Still, Pegasus was wild and refused to allow anyone to ride on his back. That honor was reserved for a true hero.

THE SNAKE-HAIRED MONSTER

The story of Pegasus begins with a beautiful woman named Medusa. She was a caretaker of the temple of Athena, the Greek goddess of wisdom. Medusa was so lovely that she attracted the attention of Poseidon, the god of the sea. Athena was very angry about the relationship. She could not do anything to a god like Poseidon, but she could punish Medusa. Athena turned the once gorgeous **mortal** into a hideous monster called a Gorgon. Medusa's long hair became a nest of hissing snakes. Her face was so ugly that anyone who looked at her turned to stone. Then Athena sent Medusa into **exile** on a faraway island.

The Greek hero Perseus was the son of Zeus and a mortal woman named Danae. The king of the land where Perseus lived sent the young hero on a mission. His task was to kill Medusa and bring back her head. Many young men had tried to accomplish the chore and had been turned to stone. But Perseus was related to Zeus, so he had help from the gods. Athena gave him a polished shield. Hermes (the messenger of the gods) gave him a sword, winged sandals, and a helmet that would make him invisible. With these gifts Perseus was able to kill Medusa by cutting off her head.

BORN FROM BLOOD

Many myths have several versions. This is true for the birth of Pegasus. In one account the winged horse leaped from Medusa's severed neck. A **variation** on this tale is that when Medusa died at the edge of the sea, her blood mixed with sea foam in the waves. Moments later Pegasus rose from the foam.

The great horse was born with a twin brother named Chrysaor. The twins did not look at all alike. Chrysaor stepped from Medusa's body as a grown man. He was a giant warrior carrying a golden spear. In another version Chrysaor was born riding on Pegasus and holding a golden sword.

The brother of Pegasus was often portrayed as a giant. He married a

According to one version of the myth, Pegasus and his brother Chrysaor leapt from Medusa's severed neck after Perseus cut off her head.

The Birth of Pegasus

naiad (a minor water goddess), and they had a son named Geryon. Also a giant, Geryon had three heads, three bodies, and a total of six arms!

Some historians who study Greek myths think that Chrysaor was just a nickname for Bellerophon, a great hero who had many adventures with Pegasus.

PEGASUS AND THE MUSES

The young winged horse was wild and spirited. For fun, he would fly high into the clouds, then swoop down over the ocean waves. Sometimes, when his hooves struck the Earth, a spring of pure water would flow from the spot. One of these springs formed at Troezen, a city southwest of Athens. Another spring formed at Peirene near the city of Corinth. Troezen and Corinth are real cities.

The goddess Athena became the protector and trainer of Pegasus. She named him after the Greek word *pegai*, which means "spring" or "well." Athena took Pegasus to stay with the nine Muses at their home on Mount Helicon, north of the Gulf of Corinth.

The Greek poet Hesiod wrote that the nine Muses were daughters of Zeus. They ruled the arts and sciences, including music, poetry, dance, and history. Urania, the muse of astronomy and universal love, accepted the job of caring for the young horse. She predicted that he would perform heroic acts. She said he would take an honored place among the stars.

Pegasus stomped on Mount Helicon to stop it from swelling with pride during a singing contest of the nine Muses. A spring of water flowed from the mountain where his hoof struck, and poets were said to gain inspiration by drinking from it.

The Birth of Pegasus

Pegasus was a favorite of the gods, from mighty Zeus to the sea god Poseidon. In fact, one day Poseidon asked Pegasus for his help. It began when nine jealous sisters challenged the nine beautiful Muses to a singing contest. The match took place on Mount Helicon. When the jealous sisters sang, the world turned dark. When the Muses sang, the world glowed and all nature stopped to listen. The song was so beautiful that even the rivers stopped flowing so they could hear it. Mount Helicon began to swell with pride. Poseidon became alarmed. He asked Pegasus to stop the mountain from rising so high.

The winged horse flew toward the ground and kicked the mountain with his hoof. He struck with such force that a crystal-clear spring burst from the spot. The spring was called the Hippocrene, or "horse spring." Its waters were said to have magical powers. Anyone who drank of them would suddenly be inspired to write great poetry. Since then Pegasus has been an inspiration for all poets.

CHAPTER 2

PEGASUS AND THE YOUNG PRINCE

Most stories claim that Bellerophon was the son of the king of Corinth. Some writers say he may have been the son of Poseidon. By the time Bellerophon was sixteen, he was known across the land as a great horseman. He had heard about the wonderful winged horse, Pegasus, and wished that he could ride him. Everyone said it was impossible. Bellerophon asked the advice of the wisest man in the city. The old man told him to sleep in the temple of Athena. Bellerophon did as he was told. He brought gifts for the goddess and asked for her help. Finally, he stretched out and went to sleep.

During the night Bellerophon had a dream that Athena visited him. She told him all about Pegasus.

She also told him that the nearby Peirene Spring was one of the great steed's favorite places to drink. Before she left, Athena placed a golden **bridle** next to the sleeping young man. In the morning Bellerophon woke to find the bridle at his side. He quickly found the spring. Pegasus was there as Athena had promised. When the horse saw the bridle, he approached gently. By using the bridle, Bellerophon became the first person to ride Pegasus.

Not long after that, Bellerophon had to flee after accidentally killing his own brother in a hunting accident. He escaped to the city of Tiryns, where he met King Proteus. Proteus became jealous of his young guest, so he came up with a plan to have him killed. He sent Bellerophon to visit Iobates, the king of Lycia, a city that is now a region in Turkey. Proteus also sent a message that Iobates should have the young man killed when he arrived. Iobates knew that killing his guest would make Zeus very angry. He did not want to risk that. Instead he sent Bellerophon on a **quest**.

The Chimera

According to myth, a terrible monster known as the Chimera regularly attacked Lycia. The beast had long, razor-sharp nails, a lion's head, a goat's body, a serpent's tail, and breath of fire. It came night after night to carry off people and livestock to its **lair**. There it would devour its victims.

Bellerophon killed the monster Chimera while riding on Pegasus.

Pegasus and the Young Prince

Iobates decided to solve his problem by sending Bellerophon to destroy the Chimera. The young hero was not afraid. On the back of mighty Pegasus, he challenged the hideous Chimera.

Even though Bellerophon and Pegasus struck from above, they could not get close to the monster because of its flaming breath. Finally Bellerophon tipped his spear with a block of lead. Pegasus flew directly at the monster. When it opened its mouth to spew fire, Bellerophon shoved the block down the Chimera's throat. Its hot breath melted the lead. The Chimera could not breathe. Bellerophon was finally able to kill it.

In one version of the story, after the Chimera died, its fiery breath could not be put out. In reality, near the valley of Olympos in Turkey there is a real place called the Chimera. Gas seeps through cracks in the Earth there, and jets of flame burn naturally amid the rocks. According to legend this valley was the very spot where the monster fell. Today the word *chimera* means any imaginary thing that appears to be made up of mismatched parts.

THE SOLYMI AND THE AMAZONS

King Iobates was pleased that the monster was dead. But he was not happy that Bellerophon and Pegasus had returned. He had hoped that the Chimera would allow him to honor the order of Proteus to kill Bellerophon, but avoid the anger of Zeus by not doing the deed himself. Iobates sent

the heroic pair on two more quests. First he asked them to conquer a warlike tribe called the Solymi. The next task was to defeat an army of female warriors known as the Amazons. Bellerophon overpowered the army by dropping boulders on them as he rode high in the sky on Pegasus's back.

The historian Herodotus wrote that the Amazons lived in a region called Sarmatia. It was a land that bordered the Black and Caspian seas and included present-day Ukraine and parts of Russia. Some modern historians think that the real Sarmatian women may have fought in battles as the men did. Those warrior women may have been the inspiration for the mythical Amazons.

BELLEROPHON'S END

Bellerophon and Pegasus returned to Lycia again. The king was so impressed with the heroes that he promised never to harm them. In fact, he offered his daughter's hand in marriage and a large gift of land to Bellerophon. At first the young man was happy with his reward. Then he began to think that he deserved more. Bellerophon decided that he should be allowed to join the gods on Mount Olympus. He slipped the golden bridle onto Pegasus and turned him toward the sky. As the two neared Olympus, Zeus sent a small biting fly to sting the winged horse and make him buck. Bellerophon was unable to hold on. He slipped from Pegasus's back and fell to Earth. Some stories

The god Zeus sent a stinging fly to cause Pegasus to buck Bellerophon off his back in midair.

say he died in the fall. Others say that Bellerophon survived but lived the rest of his life blind and crippled as punishment.

PEGASUS ON MOUNT OLYMPUS

Pegasus continued to fly upward. When he reached Olympus, Zeus welcomed him. Pegasus was given a special place in the stables of the gods. He often carried lightning and thunderbolts for Zeus. Ancient people claimed that the roll of thunder during a storm was the sound of Pegasus's hooves racing

After Pegasus came to live on Mount Olympus with the gods, he sometimes accompanied Eos, the goddess of the dawn.

across the sky. At times Eos, the goddess of dawn, rode the beautiful stallion on her morning journey.

In his later life, Pegasus took a mate named Euippe. They had one or two children, a white stallion named Celeris and perhaps a black mare named Melenippe.

IN THE NIGHT SKY

Although he was the offspring of a god, Pegasus was not immortal. As the horse neared his end, Zeus honored Pegasus by placing him in the sky as a **constellation**. Once the change was complete, one magical white feather drifted to Earth near Tarsus, a city in the modern country of Turkey. The **biblical** definition of the word *Tarsus* is "winged" or "feathered."

The rise of the constellation Pegasus in the Northern Hemisphere signals the coming of fall. Near the head of the great winged horse is a smaller constellation called Equuleus, or "little horse." It may represent Celeris, the son of Pegasus. Equuleus is the smallest constellation in the Northern Hemisphere.

CHAPTER 3

PEGASUS AND PERSEUS

As time went on, the Pegasus myth changed. In the later version, the hero Perseus is the first to ride Pegasus. European artists and poets of the **Renaissance** often represent Perseus and Pegasus together.

According to one story, Cassiopeia was the wife of Cepheus, the king of Aethiopia (or Joppa). The kingdom probably bordered the Red Sea where the modern countries of Sudan and Ethiopia exist today. Cassiopeia insulted the sea god Poseidon by bragging that her daughter, Andromeda, was more beautiful than his handmaidens, the Nereids.

Poseidon was very angry. He sent wave after wave of storms to destroy the kingdom. He also sent Cetus, a creature that was part whale and part sea monster.

21

To save his kingdom, Cepheus offered his daughter as a **sacrifice** to Cetus. She was chained to rocks near the shoreline to wait for the monster to devour her.

Meanwhile, far away, Perseus had completed his quest to kill the Gorgon Medusa. In the newer version of the myth, the hero did not use his winged sandals. Instead, when Pegasus was born, Perseus rode away on the stallion. On the journey home, the hero learned about the fate of the beautiful princess, Andromeda. He guided Pegasus to the shores of Aethiopia. The battle between Perseus and Cetus was similar to the fight between Bellerophon and the Chimera. Flying on Pegasus, Perseus attacked from above. But in this story he had a secret weapon. He had the head of Medusa in a sack. When Cetus turned to attack, Perseus pulled out the Gorgon's head and turned the monster to stone. Next he broke the beast to pieces with a blow from his sword.

Pegasus landed near the princess, and Perseus set her free. The couple was married, and Pegasus was given an honored place in the kingdom.

Red Sea Coral

Myths are often used to explain where real things come from. According to legend, after Perseus killed Cetus, he set the head of Medusa down while he washed

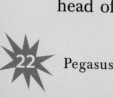

his hands in the sea. Blood from the head turned nearby seaweed to red stone, creating the first **coral**. When sea nymphs saw the beautiful formation, they caused it to spread. To this day the Red Sea is known for its amazing coral reefs.

In this painting, Perseus and Pegasus rescue Andromeda from Cetus, a sea monster sent by the angry god Poseidon to devour her.

PEGASUS IN THE SKY

The story of Perseus and Pegasus is also **immortalized** in the stars. Star groups that represent Cassiopeia, Cepheus, Perseus, and Cetus surround the constellation of Pegasus. The horse shares a star with the constellation of Andromeda. North of the equator, Pegasus rises in autumn. To an observer, the winged horse appears to be flying upside down.

Greek astronomers first named the constellation Hyppos, which means "horse." The head and neck are made up of three stars: Enif, Homan, and Matar. The main stars that make up the body are

The Pegasus and Equuleus constellations make it look like Pegasus is flying upside down.

Algenib, Scheat, Markab, and Alpheratz (shared with the constellation Andromeda). They also make up a star group called the Square of Pegasus, or the Great Square. The Greeks believed this heavenly square formed the gate to paradise. For this reason Pegasus became a symbol for the immortality of the soul. He was also thought to protect a person's spirit as it rose to the stars.

Two distant **galaxies** may be located within the constellation. The Pegasus Dwarf Irregular and the Pegasus Dwarf Spheroidal galaxies are very small and faint. They cannot be seen with the naked eye.

Ancient Beliefs

Modern astronomers recognize a belt of star groups called the zodiac. It is made up of twelve constellations known as the signs of the zodiac. Because of the movement of the Earth and the position of the stars, the Sun appears to move in a yearly path through each of these constellations. Ancient stargazers recognized 22 zodiac signs. One of those signs was Pegasus. Someone born between March 13 and April 1 was said to be born under the sign of Pegasus.

The stars that make up the Great Square were also viewed differently in ancient Greece. The four bright stars were thought to be fierce, man-eating mares that belonged to King Diomedes of Thrace. There is a legend that Bucephalus, the real horse of the leader of Macedonia, Alexander the Great, was a descendent of these mares.

Pegasus in Art

The image of Pegasus often appears on ancient pottery and metalwork. Silver and bronze Pegasus coins were used from Greece to England. These usually had Pegasus on one side and Athena, or another god or ruler, on the other.

Pegasus is also a popular subject in art. Dozens of classical painters and sculptors created scenes from the life of the winged horse. Peter Paul Rubens (1577–1640) was a Flemish painter. Pegasus appeared in at least two important paintings by Rubens. In *Perseus and Andromeda*, Pegasus's coat was a patchwork of creamy white and golden brown. In *Bellerophon Riding Pegasus Fighting the Chimaera*, the snow-white horse is seen swooping down from the sky. Bellerophon is delivering the death-blow to the monster.

Giovanni Battista Tiepolo (1696–1770) was born in Venice, Italy. He painted frescoes, which means he painted pictures on walls and ceilings in churches and palaces. Like Rubens, he created scenes of Pegasus with Bellerophon and with Perseus.

During the Renaissance, King Louis XIV of France wanted two beautiful sculptures of horses for his gardens. Antoine Coysevox (1640–1720) created two huge marble statues, *Fame Riding Pegasus* and *Mercury on Pegasus.* Today both works are in the Louvre Museum in Paris, France.

The statue Mercury on Pegasus *by Antoine Coysevox.*

Twentieth-century artists also painted the winged stallion. Best known for his portraits, John Singer Sargent (1856–1925) was an American artist. In his large oil painting *Perseus on Pegasus Slaying Medusa*, he combined several parts of the myth of the birth of Pegasus. The painting includes

Perseus, golden-winged Pegasus, Medusa, and Athena.

For French painter Odilon Redon (1840–1916), Pegasus was a favorite subject. He depicted Pegasus as a black horse. Redon also showed him with other subjects, such as battling a hydra monster or carrying a muse on his back.

A Symbol of Change

In children's literature the winged horse often represents change. The Chronicles of Narnia by C.S. Lewis is a series of seven books that takes readers to a magical world. Narnia is a land filled with witches, warriors, talking animals, and creatures of myth. There is a flying horse in *The Magician's Nephew*, the sixth book written in the series. At first he is an old, hardworking carriage horse named Strawberry. When the young main character has to travel on a quest to find a silver apple, Aslan, the lion of Narnia, turns Strawberry into a flying horse. The change includes a new name. Strawberry becomes Fledge, the father of all flying horses. In the last book of the series, *The Last Battle*, Fledge returns.

The Stravaganza series by Mary Hoffman features a flying horse in book two, *City of Stars*. The main character, Georgia, has an unhappy home life. When she buys a small statue of a winged horse, everything changes. The statue is a talisman, or magical object, that moves Georgia through space and time. She arrives at the city of Talia,

A winged horse named Fledge appears in The Chronicles of Narnia, a classic series of children's books by C.S. Lewis.

which is similar to a 16th-century city in Italy. She appears just after the birth of a flying horse, a good **omen** in Talia. Georgia begins to live between two worlds.

CHAPTER 4

PEGASUS TODAY

The myth of Pegasus has made it to the big screen. The film *Clash of the Titans* is a cult classic. It was made in 1981 and stars Harry Hamlin as Perseus. The movie blended the myths of Bellerophon and Perseus into one, then added many new elements. The sea monster, Cetus, was replaced by the Kraken, a monster from Norse mythology. The filmmakers also added a two-headed dog, a swamp monster, a monstrous vulture, and giant scorpions.

The origin of Pegasus was changed for the film. He was presented as the last of a herd of flying horses that had belonged to Zeus. For its time the special effects were very good. In some scenes a real horse

Pegasus helps Hercules in the animated Disney movie Hercules.

portrayed Pegasus. In most he was created by a mix of reality, animation, and stop-motion.

The 1997 animated Walt Disney Pictures movie *Hercules* depicted Pegasus as the hero's childhood pet. When Hercules grew up, he learned that he was the son of Zeus. With the help of Pegasus and an unhappy satyr (a goatlike creature), the young hero set out to prove himself.

Walt Disney Pictures also used flying horses in a much earlier animated film. *Fantasia* was released in 1940. It included many short stories set to classical music. In one, a family of flying horses attends a festival for Bacchus, the god of wine. The scene was set to Beethoven's Sixth Symphony. It included many creatures from Greek myth, such as centaurs, fauns, and Zeus himself.

The Small Screen

Pegasus has not been overlooked on television. In 1991 the Public Broadcasting System series *Long Ago and Far Away* aired a story called "Pegasus." It was an animated adventure about Pegasus and the Chimera. The 30-minute tale was narrated by actress Mia Farrow.

The winged horse is always in style in the world of fantasy and science fiction. Members of the *Stargate Atlantis* mission sometimes wear a Pegasus shoulder patch as part of their uniform. *Stargate Atlantis* follows the adventures of space travelers. The popular television series is set in Pegasus Galaxy.

Characters from the *Battlestar Galactica* television series wear a different Pegasus patch. This series was first shown on television in 1978. It follows the journey of the last surviving humans. They are escaping in space from an enemy that has destroyed their civilization. The main spacecraft in the series is a ship called *Galactica*, but the *Pegasus* ship was included in several episodes. The new version of the series aired in 2004. Larger and more modern than the *Galactica*, the *Pegasus* played an important role in many episodes.

TIME FOR TOYS

Beautiful and gentle Pegasus is an ideal image for toys and stuffed dolls. One of the most popular toy lines of all time is My Little Pony. Hasbro Toys introduced the cute, colorful ponies in 1982. The first six were called Earth ponies. They were quickly followed by **unicorns** and Pegasus ponies with names such as Star Flight and Firefly. The toys sold

Pegasus was featured in the DVD Barbie and the Magic of Pegasus.

very well, and Hasbro released a line of Baby Ponies, including Pegasus. Although the animated *My Little Pony* film did not do very well, the television series was a success. It had a large cast that included several of the Pegasus ponies. The line was discontinued in 1995. In 2005 the Pegasus ponies were made available again with new names like Star Catcher and Hidden Treasure.

A flying horse like Pegasus has also become the companion of the world's most fashionable doll, Barbie, from Mattel Toy Company. Barbie has held that title for half a century. She was created in 1959 by Ruth Handler. In 2005 Mattel released an animated DVD adventure, *Barbie and the Magic of Pegasus*, with Barbie as Princess Annika. In it she meets a beautiful flying horse named Brietta. Since the release of the DVD, Disney has created princess dolls, accessories, software, and a flying-horse doll that actually flaps its wings.

Mascots and Logos

The legend of Bellerophon and Pegasus is that of a great warrior who fought from the air. Pegasus willingly carried the hero aloft, and they faced the danger together. In 1941, during World War II, General Frederick Browning organized Britain's First Airborne Division. The heroic members of the division flew aloft aboard their planes to face the dangers of battle together. These young men wore a uniform shoulder patch from Greek myth.

It was Bellerophon riding Pegasus. The image clearly symbolized warriors arriving for battle by the air. The men were also known for berets they wore, which were a deep maroon color. Later the

In World War II, members of Britain's Sixth Airborne Division wore a shoulder patch on their uniforms showing Bellerophon riding Pegasus. After the division captured an important bridge, the bridge was renamed the Pegasus Bridge.

First and Sixth Airborne divisions combined. The maroon beret led to the German nickname for British airborne troops, the Red Devils.

The British Sixth Airborne Division took part in the Normandy invasion of France in the very early morning of June 5, 1944. It was the beginning of the effort to win Europe back from German forces. The paratroopers arrived by air to capture many places behind enemy lines. This included taking an important bridge over the Caen Canal. The bridge is now known as Pegasus Bridge.

A Symbol for Business

Pegasus has come to represent strength, purity, virtue, and even immortality. That makes it an excellent symbol as a business **logo** for many companies, including Reader's Digest and Pegasus Software. It is also the mascot for the University of Central Florida.

Perhaps the most beautiful logo is the Pegasus image for TriStar Pictures. The original version used in the 1980s was of Pegasus running across the screen with its wings tucked under. The horse spread his wings and leaped over the large letter T in TriStar. In 1993 the company created a new version of the logo. It had to be perfect, because it is the first thing that an audience sees at a movie. They combined a real horse and computer special effects to create a Pegasus running toward the viewer with its wings spread wide.

The Pegasus sign of Mobil Oil has become a landmark on the Magnolia Building in Dallas, Texas.

Pegasus is also the symbol of Mobil Oil. In this role he is known as Mobilis, a flying red horse. The Latin word *mobilis* means "able to be moved." The company first used the flying horse in 1911 in South Africa to represent speed and power. Mobil's Japan division was the first to color the horse red. The flying red horse was adopted as a trademark in the United States in 1931. Since then it has become a landmark in Dallas, Texas, where the Pegasus-shaped **neon** sign rides high atop the Magnolia Building. The structure was the Texas headquarters of the Magnolia Petroleum Company, and, later, the Mobil Oil Company. It is currently the Magnolia Hotel. The original symbol was placed there in 1934. A restored version of the original Pegasus was dedicated at midnight on December 31, 1999, to celebrate the year 2000. The 1934 sign is on display at the Dallas Farmer's Market.

PEGASUS ON THE MOVE

In 1948 Rollie Free was known for breaking the American motorcycle land speed record. On a motorcycle called Black

Lightning, he reached a speed of over 150 miles per hour (241kph) at the Bonneville Salt Flats in Utah. One of his sponsors was Mobil Oil, and the Mobil logo of Pegasus was on the gas tank of his motorcycle. The motorcycle was made to be as light as possible. Steel parts were replaced with lightweight aluminum. Parts that were not very important were removed. The most unusual part of the event was that Rollie

The Pegasus rocket became the first privately developed space launch vehicle.

Free rode the entire distance lying flat on his stomach. He also wore a bathing suit so that his clothes would not create wind resistance.

In 1990 the three-stage Pegasus rocket became the world's first privately developed space launch vehicle. It was developed by Orbital Sciences Corporation. The Pegasus is used to launch small satellites into low Earth orbit. Pegasus is carried upward over open ocean by a traditional aircraft. At about 40,000 feet (12,192m), it is dropped. A few seconds later, the first stage rocket motor fires and Pegasus boosts the satellite into position.

Pegasus at Sea

Pegasus is an inspiration for poets. The Pegasus Project has become an inspiration for children. Since 1994 more than 4,000 young people have been able to participate in the project. As passengers on a 51-foot (15.54m) sailing vessel, they explore the San Francisco Bay. The participants learn about the geology, history, weather, and marine environment of the bay. The young sailors also learn to chart a course.

The Journey of Pegasus

From ancient times to the present, Pegasus has changed in many ways. He has multiplied into herds of winged pegasi and hordes of cute toys. The name Pegasus no longer means an immaculate white horse. He may be black, gold, silver, or pink.

Pegasus

He has changed patterns and size and even taken on traits of the unicorn. A flying horse with a horn is referred to as either an Alicorn or a Pegacorn.

For hundreds of years, Pegasus has captured the imaginations of adults and children alike. Many would like to believe that he is more than a myth. So the question remains. Can horses fly? Perhaps the answer is in the night sky. On a crisp autumn evening one only has to look up to see Pegasus glittering high above.

Glossary

biblical: Relating to the Bible.

bridle: Leather straps, bit, and reins fitted for control of a horse's head.

constellation: A group of stars that forms a pattern visible from Earth.

coral: A marine life-form that lives in colonies and has an external skeleton.

exile: Being sent away from one's home unwillingly.

galaxies: Groups of billions of stars and their planets, moons, gases, and dust.

immortal: Undying, eternal.

immortalized: To be represented in a way that makes one famous for a very long time.

lair: A retreat or hideaway for a wild animal.

logo: A recognizable image or design that represents an organization or company.

mortal: Someone having a limited lifespan.

mythology: A collection of myths, stories, or beliefs, which are not necessarily true, about a culture, place, or individual.

naturalist: Somebody who studies or is interested in nature, including the history of plants and animals.

neon: A colorless gas that glows in bright colors when electricity is passed through it.

omen: A sign or warning about an event that will take place in the future.

quest: A mission or journey in search of something.

Renaissance: The period in European history from the 14th through 16th centuries.

sacrifice: A ritual offering to appease a god.

traditional: Time-honored or customary.

unicorns: Mythical horses with a single horn on the forehead.

variation: A difference between things that are otherwise alike.

For Further Exploration

Books

Heather Amery, *Greek Myths for Young Children*. London: Usborne, 2000. This 128-page book covers many of the most important Greek myths and features Pegasus on the cover.

Hestia Evans, *Mythology*. Somerville, MA: Candlewick, 2007. A primer on Greek myths with pop-ups, flaps, crafts, and other surprises. With plenty of great information, this volume is from the popular Ologies series.

Dorothy Hoopes and Ned Evslin, *The Greek Gods*. New York: Scholastic, 1995. A reference to have on hand when reading Greek myths. Each god is described clearly, and the functions of each are explained.

Jane Mason, *The Flying Horse*. New York: Grosset & Dunlap, 1999. A brief but complete telling of Pegasus's quest with Bellerophon in an early reader format. It includes beautiful illustrations.

Marianna Mayer, *Pegasus*. New York: Mayer & Craft, 1998. This classic story of Pegasus and

Bellerophon is simply told. It highlights the bond between the two heroic figures. The beautiful illustrations are oil over watercolor.

INDEX

Long Ago and Far Away (TV series), 32
Louis XIV (French king), 26

M
The Magician's Nephew (Lewis), 28
Mascots, Pegasus as, 34–36
Medusa, 7–8, 22–23
Mercury on Pegasus (Coysevox), 26
Mobil Oil, 38
Muses, 10, 12
My Little Pony (toy line), 33–34
Mythology, 5. *See* Greek mythology; Norse mythology
Myths, 4
  purpose of, 22

N
Norse mythology, 5

P
Pegacorn, 41
Pegasus, 5, 7
  in art, 21, 26–28
  becomes constellation, 20, 24
  changing depictions of, 40–41
  in films/TV shows, 30–32
  as inspiration for poets, 12
  in mascots/logos, 34–40
  on Mount Olympus, 19–20
  symbolism of, 25
  variations on birth of, 8, 10
Pegasus Project, 40
Perseus (Greek hero), 7–8, 21
  battle between Cetus and, 22

star groups representing, 24
Perseus and Andromeda (Rubens), 26
Perseus on Pegasus Slaying Medusa (Sargent), 27–28
Pliny the Elder (Roman historian), 4
Poseidon (god of the sea), 7, 12, 21–22
Proteus (king of Tiryns), 14

R
Redon, Odilon, 28
Rubens, Peter Paul, 26

S
Sargent, John Singer, 27
Solymi (warlike tribe), 17
Square of Pegasus, 25
Stargate Atlantis (TV series), 32
Surya (Hindu sun god), 5

T
Tarkshya, 5
Tiepolo, Giovanni Battista, 26
TriStar Pictures, 36

U
Urania (muse), 10

Z
Zeus (ruler of Greek gods), 5, 7, 17, 19
  daughters of, 10
  Pegasus honored by, 20
Zodiac, 25

Picture Credits

About the Author

Q.L. Pearce has written more than 100 trade books for children and more than 30 classroom workbooks and teacher manuals on the topics of reading, science, math, and values. Pearce has written science-related articles for magazines; regularly gives presentations at schools, bookstores, and libraries; and is a frequent contributor to the educational program of the Los Angeles County Fair. She is assistant regional advisor for The Society of Children's Book Writers and Illustrators in Orange, San Bernardino, and Riverside Counties in Southern California.